Alfred Stieglitz

Annual salon and exhibition of amateur photography

catalogue [1st]

Alfred Stieglitz

Annual salon and exhibition of amateur photography
catalogue [1st]

ISBN/EAN: 9783743432741

Manufactured in Europe, USA, Canada, Australia, Japa

Cover: Foto ©Thomas Meinert / pixelio.de

Manufactured and distributed by brebook publishing software
(www.brebook.com)

Alfred Stieglitz

Annual salon and exhibition of amateur photography

FOURTH
ANNUAL
SALON
& EXHIBITION
AMATEUR
PHOTOGRAPHY

CATALOGUE

FOURTH ANNUAL SALON AND EXHIBITION *of Amateur* Photography *held at* *CASE LIBRARY* Cleveland, *November 20 to December 2*

1 8 9 9

COMMITTEE OF ARRANGEMENTS
1899

R. P. CATTRALL
W. T. HIGBEE
MISS JEAN T. CHAPIN
F. N. CLELAND
CHARLES ORR

The judges shall consist of two artists and a photographer and shall be appointed by the Librarian and known only to him. The awards shall consist of certificates of equal value, for superior excellence, and honorable mention for merit.

The Exhibition shall consist of six classes, namely:

CLASS A. Portrait and Figure Studies not made in a professional studio.

CLASS B.
1 Landscapes.
2 Marines.
3 Clouds.

CLASS C. Animal Studies.

CLASS D. Flower and Fruit Studies.

CLASS E.
1 Architecture.
2 Interiors.
3 Machinery and Manufactured Objects.

CLASS F. A Set of two or more pictures telling a complete story.

339   DAWN   Carle E. Semon

CATALOGUE

Abbott, C. Yarnall

10 South Eighteenth Street, Philadelphia, Pa.

1   Summer
2   " Virginia "
3   Study of a Head
4   " Herodias "
5   " Marie "
6   " Dryad "

Albaugh, H. M.

29 Euclid Avenue, Cleveland, O.

7   Interior of Sawmill, Zoar, O.
8   Dreaming of Other Days
9   A Glimpse of the Tuscarawas
10   The Passing Storm
11   Below the Flour Mill
12   The Boat Landing
13   An August Morning
14   Along the Ohio Canal
15   Peaceful Valley, near Zoar Station, O.
16   A Corner in J. D. Rockefeller's Park
17   Alex. Gunn's Cottage, Zoar
18   A Mansion in Zoar
19   Along the Towpath
20   Old Church at Zoar
21   Shadows on the Canal

Appel, D.

62 Holyoke Place, Cleveland, O.

22   An Outdoor Portrait
23   In the Cornfield
24   Recreation
25   Turkish Dancing Girl
26   A Day Dream
27   An Oriental Beauty

Baker, F. C.

522 Hickox Building, Cleveland, O.

28 Winter Landscape
29 Landscape
30   "
31   "
32 Marine View
33 Haystacks
34 The Willow Tree
35 Landscape
36 Calves
37 Landscape

Baldwin, Mr. and Mrs. S. Prentiss

736 Prospect Street, Cleveland, O.

38 The Mountains in Rain
39 A Gathering Storm
40 Clearing
41 Closing Day
42 Rocky Mountains from the Garden of the Gods
43 A Summer Day
44 A Village Mill
45 Nelson's Ledge, Parkman, O.
46 Williams Cañon, Colorado
47 Lengthening Shadows
48 Pike's Peak
49 Drifting Clouds
50 A Den
51 An Upper Hall
52 The South Porch

Bates, Charles F.

2642 Euclid Avenue, Cleveland, O.

53 "Alas, poor Yorick"
54 Portrait of Mrs. B.
55 "Doña Ysabel"
56 "Indecision"

Bradley, L. C.

90 Van Ness Avenue, Cleveland, O.

57 A Basket of Kittens
58 A Pair of Thoroughbreds
59 Sunset on the Gulf of Mexico
60 Hotel Bellevue at Bellaire, Florida
61 Old Spanish Gates, St. Augustine, Florida
62 Early Autumn
63 Forest and Stream
64 An Enchanting Spot
65 On Old Huron
66 The Glens, Berea, O.

Buss, Charles M.

53 Collins Place, Cleveland, O.

67 Steamer " North West " leaving Lock
68 Bridge in Belle Isle Park, Detroit, Michigan

Cattrall, R. P.

383 Amesbury Avenue, Cleveland, O.

69 Sturgeon Point
70 Homeward Bound
71 The Wreath
72 Happy Memories
73 Preparing for a Walk
74 The Althea

Chapin, Miss Jean T.

1160 East Madison Avenue, Cleveland, O.

75 The Town of Gorcum, Holland
76 Watch Tower near Salerno, Italy
77 Bellagio, Lake Como, Italy
78 Venice
79 The Cappucini Monastery at Amalfi, Italy
80 Bank of the Reuss, Lucerne, Switzerland

A Christmas Journey

The Lake Shore & Michigan Southern Ry.

"Recognized to be the finest in the United
States, in point of roadbed, equipment and sevice."

71 THE WREATH

Chew, W. B.

Xenia, O.

81 The Michigan Flyer
82 The Diver, Bay View, Michigan
83 A Sheep Study, Walloon Lake, Mich.
84 A Northern Michigan Trout Stream
85 A Rough Day
86 Eventide, near Bay View, Mich.
87 Stormy Weather Bay

Clark, Geo. A.

417 Jennings Avenue, Cleveland, O.

88 The Mountain Stream
89 "But Now the Mill Wheel's Silent"
90 On a Summer's Day
91 An "Arcadia" Cottage Living Room
92 Barbara's Cottage
93 June
94 At Sundown

Cleland, F. N.

40 Brenton Street, Cleveland, O.

95 A Suburban Home—Looking East
96 A Suburban Home—Looking West
97 An Interior
98 A Marine View
99 A Hill Road
100 Niagara—American Falls From Steamer "Maid of the Mist"
101 The Parting of the Ways
102 Niagara—American Falls
103 The Lone Fisherman
104 A Little Fisher Maiden
105 When Evening Shadows Gather Round
106 A Smoker
107 Go !
108 Coming
109 Going
110 A Bit of the Backyard

THE HELMAN-TAYLOR COMPANY

cordially invite you to visit their Store and Art Galleries.

NEW BOOKS are constantly being received from the Publishers. You will always find the latest publications as well as the standard works.

The Stationery Department is complete in every respect.

New patterns and tints in Note Papers.

New designs in Engraving,

New styles of Cards,

Desk Ornaments, Blotters, Pens.

ART DEPARTMENT

You will find a treat in store for you among the beautiful pictures.

Soule Photographs,

Carbon Prints,

Baryto Prints,

Allinari Views,

Plaster Casts,

Medallions, Etc.

CIRCULATING LIBRARY

All the latest Fiction. This invitation is extended to everyone.

THE HELMAN-TAYLOR CO.

23-25-27 Euclid Ave.,

near the Square.

Clement, F. R.

81 Aiken Avenue, Cleveland, O.

111 Vacation Days
112 The Mahoning
113 American Falls, Niagara

Clement, Mrs. F. R.

81 Aiken Avenue, Cleveland, O.

114 Cousins
115 Just One Peach
116 Curly Locks
117 A Basket of Mischief
118 An Unconscious Pose
119 Good Morning

Cobb, L. N.

23 Brevier Street, Cleveland, O.

120 Detroit Water Works Tower and Flower Clock
121 Watching for Papa
122 Watch Maker's Bench
123 "Take our Pictures on the Old Wagon"
124 Landscape Scene along the Cuyahoga
125 A Spot for Reflections—Ohio Canal
126 Landscape Scene at Bedford, O.
127 Landscape Scene in the Woods
128 View in Gordon Park

Corne, L. F.

76 State Street, Boston, Mass.

129 Dennison Road, Annisquam
130 Peel Quay, Isle of Man
131 Across the Charles to Cambridge
132 Squam River
133 Twilight at Annisquam
134 Portrait of a Child
135 Portrait
136 Bruges, Evening

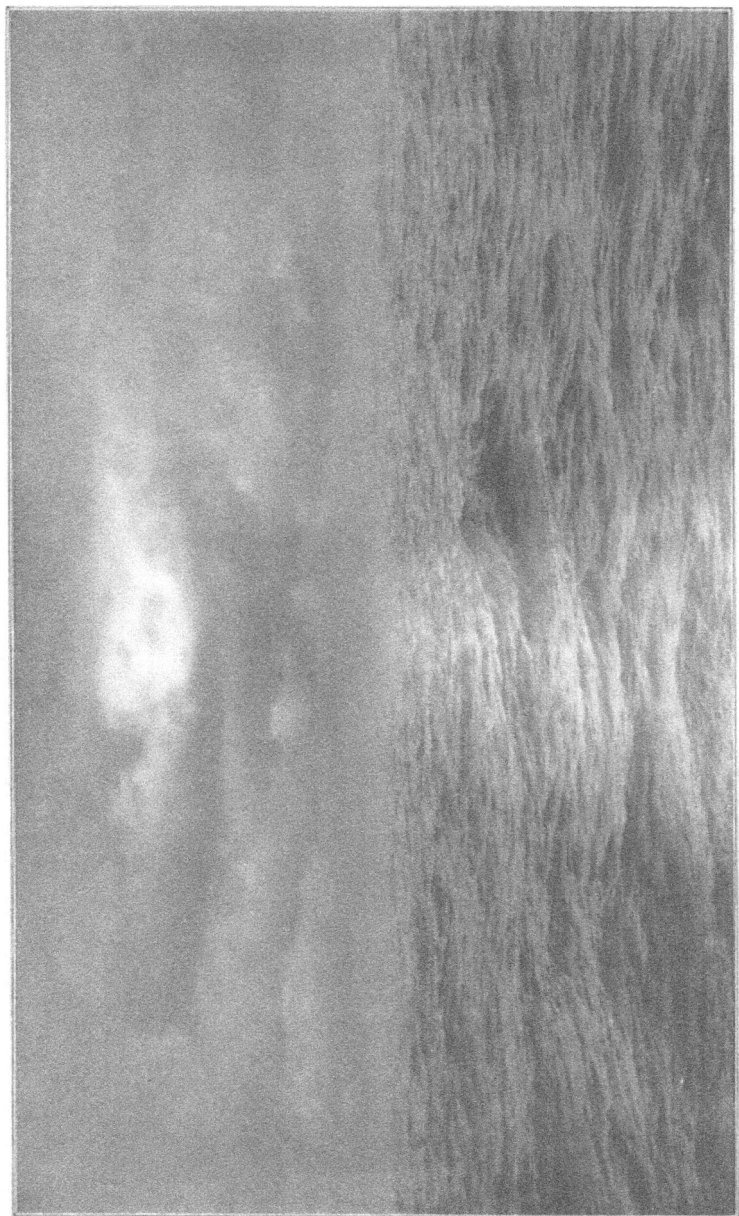

Engraved by Samuel K. Mason, Cleveland.

32 MARINE

F. C. Baker

Cornell, A. E.

148 Taylor Street, Cleveland, O.

137 Drive in Riverside Cemetery
138 Rustic Bridge, Edgewater Park
139 Riverside Drive
140 Edgewater Boulevard

Crosier, Miss Josephine

1052 First Avenue, Cleveland, O.

141 Gordon Park
142 Landscape
143 Woodland Avenue
144 " Sleepy (K) nittie "
145 Landscape
146 Outdoor Portraiture
147 " City of Erie "
148 Portraits
149 Varnish Tank Room
150 Landscape

Day, F. Holland

9 Pinckney Street, Boston, Mass.

151 The Seven Last Words of Christ
152 Coronna
153 Young Daphnis
154 Menelik (a fragment)
155 Beatrice
156 Nubia
157 Somnolence
158 Portrait of Mrs. K.
159 The Trumpeter
160 Italian Girl
161 Beauty is Truth, Truth Beauty
162 The Crucifixion

Dean, J. E.

192 Perry Street, Cleveland, O.

163 June Roses

Western
Reserve
Building

SUPERIOR COR. WATER STREET

This Building will be enlarged during the coming year; 75 additional office rooms.

Application for space can be made to

S. A. RAYMOND, Room 710.

CLARENCE
BUILDING
122 Euclid Avenue

Engraved by Samuel R. Mason, Cleveland.

Emerine, Andrew—continued

194 The Artist
195 " Dorothy "
196 The Milkmaid
197 The Truants
198 Trudging Home
199 At the Beach, Lake Erie
200 " Ship a hoy !''

Gaehr, A. J.

95 St. Clair Street, Cleveland, O.

201 Cascade Park, New Castle, Pa.
202 " Reflections "
203 Along Neshannock River

Guest, Mrs. Fred. C.

1121 Lorain Street, Cleveland, O.

204 Fairmount Street Scene
205 Boulevard Scene

Hatch, Homer B.

66 Plymouth Street, Cleveland, O.

206 The Abandoned Mill, Zoar, O.
207 Where Wavelets Ripple, Tuscarawas River, Zoar
208 A Summer Morning on the Tuscarawas, Zoar
209 " I Pescatori," Tuscarawas River
210 " The Raging Canal," Zoar
211 Lock on the Ohio Canal, near Bolivar

Hawthorne, Miss Ruth

1 The Martin, Milwaukee, Wis.

212 West Park, Milwaukee, Wis.
213 Downes College, Milwaukee, Wis.
214 Milwaukee Bay
215 Beach at Whitefish Bay

The
Cowell and Hubbard
Company

Jewelry and Kindred Lines

Euclid Avenue Corner Bond Street
Cleveland, Ohio

Franklin Book Bindery

224 CHAMPLAIN STREET

CLEVELAND, O.

LIBRARY, MAGAZINE
AND FINE BINDING

BLANK BOOKS TO ORDER

Higbee, W. T.

240 Superior Street, Cleveland, O.

- 208½   In the Adirondacks
- 209½   An Evening Sky
- 210½   Berrying
- 211½   Sweet Peas. Miss H.
- 212½   In the Garden
- 213½   Waiting for the Cows
- 214½   The Farmer's Children
- 215½   A Birch Swamp

Hildebran, W. G.

9 The Baker, Cleveland, O.

- 216   Fallen Branches
- 217   Quietude
- 218   A Woodland Study in Light and Shade
- 219   Eventide
- 220   A Woodland Path
- 221   The Babbling Brook

Hyde, A. Lincoln

816 New England Building

- 222   Hartford Memorial Arch
- 223   Zero Frost
- 224   The Forgers
- 225   After the Shower
- 226   Bright Spring Morning
- 227   'Twixt Forest and Farm

Kelly, L. A.

25 Vienna Street, Cleveland, O.

- 228   Sheep
- 229   The Hillside Path
- 230   Danger Ahead
- 231   The Rising Moon
- 232   The Shepherd and His Flock
- 233   A Canadian Home
- 234   Along the Muskoka River
- 235   The Indian Basket Makers

THE "GORGE" affords
photographers unusual op-
portunities for procuring
good pictures both in the
winter and summer sea-
sons.   The scenery is wild
and picturesque, combin-
ing fine tree, water and
road effects. . . . .
Take the AKRON, BEDFORD
& CLEVELAND Electric Cars.

161 " BEAUTY IS TRUTH, TRUTH BEAUTY " F. Holland Day

Krebs, Carl
429 Woodland Avenue, Cleveland, O.

236 River Bottoms
237 Stepping Stones
238 At the Brookside
239 May
240 Playmates
241 Parting of a November Day
242 Carving Dewey's Name
243 Felines' Friend
244 Black River
245 Winter Sport
246 Cornfield
247 A Work of Nature
248 Flowering Magnolia
249 Cryptogramic Vegetation
250 In the Wilds of Tinker's Creek
251 A Basket of Mushrooms
252 A Bouquet of Winter Twigs
253 The Botanist's Booty
254 Cecropia Moth
255 *Flowering Shadbush, Parma Creek
256 *Waterfalls at Black River
257 *Geauga Lake
258 *On the Banks of the Grand River
259 *Wild Scenery at Parma Creek
260 *Swamp Vegetation; Orchids

Lee, George E.
4 Quimby Place, Cleveland, O.

261 Landscape
262 The Forty-foot Hole, Elyria, O.
263 Near the Lower Boulevard
264 Landscape
265 Flood's Rock, Elyria
266 Black River, Elyria
267 Beach, Gordon Park
268 The Boulevard
269 Black River, Elyria

*Not Competing

Lee, George E.—continued

   270 The West Falls, Elyria

   271 River Scene, Elyria

   272 Lower Boulevard

   273 The Cave, Elyria

McGeorge, John

     286 Genesee Avenue, Cleveland, O.

   274 Wade Park Lake

   275 Landscape

   276 Landscape

   277 Perry's Monument

   278 Landscape

Mergenthaler, A. E.

     Fostoria, O.

   279 The Mower

   280 Daughter of Simonides

   281 Crack the Whip

Moore, C. G.

     Lisbon, O.

   282 The Greed of Gold

   283 The Pride of the Harem

   284 "Who Would Not be Infirm and Aged to be Consoled Like Me."

   285 Seeking Solace

   286 A Mountain Road

Newberry, A. St. J.

     41 Atwater Building, Cleveland, O.

   287 Falls, Hillbrook,   The Adirondacks

   288 Shore of Meacham Lake,   "

   289 Fly Catching, Buck Pond,   "

   290 Foot of Rapids, St. Regis River, "

   291 Head of Rapids, St. Regis River, "

   292 Shore of Meacham Lake,   "

   293 Cottage, St. Hubert's Inn,   "

Newman, Louis

     Plain Dealer Office, Cleveland, O.

   294 Ready for the Walk

IF THERE BE any advantage in study amid refined, wholesome surroundings,

where one must

Be Thorough,

where educational

. . aims prevail,

It would be wise to attend The Central Institute.

Attendance never so large nor of so high grade scholarship as to-day.

The Central Institute,
Willson-Scovill.

Branches taught:

Bookkeeping,	College Preparatory,
Shorthand,	Higher Mathematics,
English,	German,
Mechanical Drawing,	French.

Engraved by Samuel R. Mason, Cleveland

64   AN ENCHANTING SPOT   L. C. Bradley

Olmsted, Mrs. Helen B.
649 Prospect Street, Cleveland, O.
- 295 Mary's Garden
- 296 Where Oranges Grow

Page, J. H.
357 Bolton Avenue, Cleveland, O.
- 297 Bedford Bridge Through the Tree Tops.
- 298 Ruin of Shaker Mill-dam
- 299 Valley of Conneaut Creek
- 300 A Windy Morning, Gordon Park

Paine, H. E.
367 Amesbury Avenue, Cleveland, O.
- 301 A Cleveland Home
- 302 Portraits
- 303 A Club Library
- 304 A Bit of Catalina Island

Peck, Hobart F.
Akron, O.
- 305 Portrait Study

Petersilge, Emil
314 Woodland Avenue, Cleveland, O.
- 306 Bedford Glens
- 307 "   "
- 308 Canadian Falls
- 309 Minnowing in Tinker's Creek

Potter, F. P.
64 Glen Park Place, Cleveland, O.
- 310 Ghosts of Summer
- 311 Near to Nature's Heart
- 312 Twilight
- 313 Ruins of Outer Wall, Newgate Prison, Newgate, Connecticut
- 314 Ruins of Prison Ship,   "   "   "   "
- 315 The Hush of Noonday, Milford, Connecticut
- 316 Chess Players—"Mate"
- 317 Looking East from the New England Building
- 318 Motherless
- 319 The Evening Prayer

THE CITIZENS SAVINGS AND LOAN ASSOCIATION

CLEVELAND, OHIO.

CAPITAL STOCK,	$1,000,000.00
SURPLUS FUND, .	1,000,000.00
UNDIVIDED PROFITS,	202,312.00
DEPOSITS, .	8,409,944.79

FREDERICK W. PELTON, President

GEORGE W. HOWE
Vice-President

HORACE B. CORNER
Secretary and Treasurer

H. W. LUETKEMEYER
Vice-President

ORLO C. NELSON,
Assistant Treasurer

DIRECTORS

FREDERICK W. PELTON
WM. BINGHAM
H. W. LUETKEMEYER
KAUFMAN HAYS
E. T. HAMILTON
LATHROP COOLEY
GEO. W. HOWE
W. B. CHISHOLM
E. P. WRIGHT
J. M. JONES
S. T. EVERETT
E. R. PERKINS
R. McLAUCHLAN
BENJAMIN ROSE
GEO. H. WORTHINGTON

J. H. WADE
CHARLES W. BINGHAM
STILES H. CURTISS
HENRY C. RANNEY
DOUGLAS PERKINS
HORACE B. CORNER
DAVID Z. NORTON
W. D. REES
SAMUEL MATHER
N. B. PRENTICE
BELDEN SEYMOUR
J. V. PAINTER
GEO. A. GARRETSON
ORLO C. NELSON
HARRY R. EDWARDS

Potter, F. P.—continued

Art in Printing

It is knowing *where* to put the paint, and how much, and what colors that makes the true artist. It is knowing *where* to put the ink, and how much, and what colors that makes the competent printer. The right use of printing facilities is our constant study and practice. . . . . We are making a specialty of small work for commercial and other purposes. We invite test orders from those who appreciate technical skill in the production of their printed matter to determine whether it is not better to use this than the kind they have been using. All printing is cheap which fully accomplishes its purpose; all which falls short of its purpose is dear at any price.

E. T. Smith & Co.

16 Middle Street, cor. High

Telephone Main 3075-J

Cleveland

402　"MATILDA."　　　　　Henry S. Upson.

Sholes, F. T.—continued

Shumaker, C. R.

Creston, O.

Smith, A. L.

37 Kenwood Street, Cleveland, O.

Smith, Raymond A.

1198 East Madison Avenue, Cleveland, O.

Smith, Mrs. Wilson G.

156 Taylor Street, Cleveland, O.

Smith, Mrs. Wilson G.—continued

 376 An Indian Graveyard
 377 F. W. Simmons' Studio at Mackinac
 378 Net Houses, Charlevoix, Michigan
 379 A Wilderness Waterway
 380 "So Boss"
 381 "When the Tide Comes in"
 382 Indians at Cross Village

Steven, H. Fairchild
   152 Broadway, N. Y.
 383 Broadway from a 26th Story Balcony
 384 Twenty-foot Frontage on Ann St. Park Row Building, N. Y.

Turnbull, W. C.
   485 Russell Avenue, Cleveland, O.
 385 The parting Ways
 386 One of Nature's Decorations
 387 In the Gloaming
 388 Bridge at Rocky River
 389 After the First Snowfall
 390 "I Like my Bath"
 391 "Look! Mamma, I'm habin my Picture Took"
 392 In Ye Olden Time
 393 Portrait of Miss S.
 394 One of our Commerce Carriers

Upham, Mrs. C. F.
   236 Superior Street, Cleveland, O.
 395 Flock of Sheep
 396 Waterfall, Wade Park
 397 Log Cabin, Wade Park
 398 Public Square
 399 Bridge, Edgewater Park
 400 Lake, Wade Park

Upson, Henry S.
   514 New England Building, Cleveland, O.
 401 Battle Monument, West Point, N. Y.
 402 "Matilda" (Flashlight Portrait)
 403 Cullom Memorial Building, West Point, N. Y.

Watson, Miss Eva Lawrence
10 South Eighteenth Street, Philadelphia, Pa.
404 Portrait of Two Children

405 Child's Portrait

406 Miss H. and "Jack"

407 "La Renaissance"

408 Study

White, Clarence H.
161 North Fifth Street, Newark, O.
*409 The Black Shawl

*410 The Tower

*411 Interlude

*412 Fear

*413 Profile Study

*414 Sabbath Morning

*415 On the Old Stair

*416 Perplexity

Whitman, F. P.
Adelbert College, Cleveland, O.
417 October Weeds

Whitney, R. W.
236 Superior Street, Cleveland, O.
418 S. Andrew's House

419 Interior

420 "Ben"

421 Oldest House in Cleveland, O.

422 Portrait

423 Portrait Enlarged

Williams, W. M.
46 Holyoke Place, Cleveland, O.
424 Above the Falls

425 An October Day on Goat Island

426 A Beauty Spot at Niagara

427 The Old Castle

428 A Stray Stream from the Upper Rapids

429 The Pride of the Dairy

Winsor, Mrs. Q. J.
649 Prospect Street, Cleveland, O.
430 His First Over-alls

*Not Competing

53   " ALAS, POOR YORICK "

www.ingramcontent.com/pod-product-compliance
Lightning Source LLC
Chambersburg PA
CBHW020254290326
41930CB00039B/1402